AF 243768

From the collection:

A Complex Release of Pain

"Connections"

"Words On A Moving Page"

"Cigarettes and Candyfloss"

"Beautiful"

"Cherry"

Contents

Introduction

The action takes place anywhere, at any time. The main focus of the play is the connections between all of the characters. The connection between Sam and Sarah is the principal and most important connection of the play.

The connection Sam and Sarah have with each other is complex. Sam and Sarah have been in a relationship for four years and are engaged to be married. Sam and Sarah are comfortable with each other and depend on each other, as they share an apartment – Sam has a well-paid job, while Sarah attends university. They are comfortable with each other's families, and this partly leads to the two rarely questioning the security of their relationship and whether it is right for them. Their actions are not always perfect.

The purpose of the play is not to delve deeply into these actions, as the connection is what holds the two together despite the questionable actions committed by either of the two characters. The point of the play arises from the modern state of society and the constant shift to assign blame and define what is acceptable and correct in the modern world. People tend to focus on labelling others as "good" or "bad" and engage in cancel culture, failing to consider the situation, context, personal well-being, or lives of ordinary people.

The idea of the play is to highlight the flawed nature of this ideology of modern society. We are all just people; I believe the world is not black and white, and those lines are blurred. There are no distinct "good" or "bad" sides, or people in society – we are all the same, and the constant blaming and finger-pointing is a negative aspect of the modern world.

Focusing on the connections between people, rather than solely on their actions, can significantly improve how we treat others. No one can help whom they love; the connection will always be present, no matter how hard a person tries to resist it. Therefore, by focusing on connections between people in a romantic or platonic way, society and the modern world may become happier and more peaceful, free from judgement and pervasive hate. That is the key message of *Connections*.

Actions committed by Sam and Sarah are questionable in terms of the morals of these characters, raising debates about whether they are "good" people. According to the ideology of the modern world, these characters and their traits may not be deemed acceptable. However, the play focuses on the connection and genuine love they have for each other. Sam and Sarah both feel deep love for one another, depend on each other, and want the best for each other. They are both troubled, depending on family and friends for support. It's these connections that are important in the play and valuable in everyday life.

Connections serves as a reminder to cherish the connections you have with your close friends and family and to value those relationships – not to scrutinise every action, but to consider what they mean to you and the significance of the connection you share. Analysing those connections and relationships and understanding their true meaning can greatly help a person mature and be more thankful.

Talking and spending time with the people who matter most and appreciating the moment is becoming less common in the modern world. Being thankful for those moments and those connections is what the play is all about. This message of self-worth and respect is often overlooked in modern relationships and is exemplified in the relationship between Sam and Sarah.

Rationality, logic, and self-worth are unbalanced in their relationship, intentionally so, to show that sometimes relationships are messy, and although people may be connected – the timing may not be right, and the relationship may need to end.

All the ideologies and messages of the play are intentionally personified and brought to life through the complex and messy relationship of Sam and Sarah in *Connections*.

Connections suggests that relationships don't always make sense. Often, no one is at fault, and the relationship simply breaks down. It's natural to blame yourself or the other person. I want to emphasise that both parties in the relationship are flawed, as is very much the case with Sam and Sarah. But that doesn't mean they're bad or wrong. They're just human, making human mistakes, as we all do.

-T

Settings

The action of the play *can* be transposed to any place, at any time period.

ACT ONE: *Midday in Sam's apartment, the local town later in the afternoon, Sarah's family home the same night.*

ACT TWO: *The same night in Sam's apartment, later in the night at the local pub, the smoking area of the local pub longer into the night, past midnight in a side street close to the local pub.*

ACT THREE: *A month later, in a counselling office in the local town, Sarah's family home later that afternoon, the smoking area of the local pub around midnight, a week later in Sam's apartment.*

The Characters

SAM BROWN *(the boy)*

A seemingly nice, tall young man. He is well dressed, to cover dark secrets of his own. He has a hard and difficult past he wishes to overcome and struggles to handle his emotions. When emotional, he always seems to be on the edge.

SARAH REID *(the girl)*

Sarah is well put together. She is well mannered, polite, and kind. She is confused on her relationship with Sam because of his actions of a recent summer and questions his morality. When emotional, she loses all control and cannot control what she says.

ANNIE JENNINGS *(the best friend)*

Annie is Sarah's emotional support; they have been friends for years. Longer than Sam and Sarah's relationship. She is kind and witty and will always stick up for Sarah.

JOHN SMYTH *(the best friend)*

Tall, funny, and seemingly stupid. John helps Sam through the darkest periods of his life through his comic relief. With Sarah trying to sabotage their friendship; John is always there for Sam and will always succeed in cheering him up as their bond will never break.

TONY GRAHAM *(the long-time friend)*

Tony and Sam have been friends since they were four, but time and the process of life has drifted them apart. But that never fails to completely tear their connection. Tony and Sam always reconnect and are always there for each other when it matters the most.

LUKE WILLIAMS *(the complexity)*

Luke is Sarah's crush of the last summer. Luke is the man that can always get under Sam's skin. Spiralling him into mania, and insane decisions. Creating problems in Sarah and Sam's relationship.

FIONA REID *(the mother)*

Sarah's mother. Sarah and Fiona are incredibly close, and the pair are inseparable. Fiona will not let anything hurt Sarah in the long term and will always be there to protect her.

TODD REID *(the father)*

Witty and clueless, Sarah's father always has her feelings as his main concern. Although he his good friends with Sam, he will always think of Sarah as his number one priority.

NATHAN REID *(the brother)*

Young and innocent, the only thing that matters to Nathan is his sister, Sarah.

RYAN KIDD *(a close friend)*

Sam's good friend. Ryan provides a much-needed distraction and companionship in Sam's life.

LAURA BAXTER *(a close friend)*

A friend always ready to help Sarah in need.

DOCTOR ADAMS *(a helpful therapist)*

Comforting and understanding. Sam's therapist helps him through times of need.

JASON REID *(the brother)*

Much older than Sarah and tired from his hard job. Jason helps Sarah in heightened states.

VIOLET BROWN *(the sister)*

Older than Sam and his motherly figure. Sam's sister is always there to pick up the pieces when he crumbles.

For

Jack

First published in 2024

By TM Publishings.

Printed in the United Kingdom.

All Rights Reserved.

© TM Publishings, 2025

Actors on cover:

Ella Kilpatrick

Jackson Allen

ISBN 978-1-0682436-0-8

Tom Moore
Connections

TM

Connections, a production written by Tom Moore and produced by TM Publishings. First performed at the Ballyearl Courtyard Theatre for a One Night Only performance on the 9th August 2024. The cast is as follows:

Sam – Jack Cairns
Sarah – Tait Brennan
Doctor Adams – Iona Holt
Annie – Ella Kilpatrick
John – Matthew Mullan
Tony – Jackson Allen
Luke – Joseph Golden
Todd – Tom Moore
Ryan – Rhys Pollard

Directed by **Tom Moore**
Written by **Tom Moore**
Assistant Directed by **Megan Muldoon**

Set built by **Andrew Moore**
Photography by **Debbie Muldoon**

PRODUCED BY
TM PUBLISHINGS

Act One

Scene one

The rain pours on a bleak night. Water trickles from either side of the stage. A kitchen scene is presented centre stage. There is a large screen placed at the cyclorama. There is a moment. A rainy street scene appears on the screen. The words "Connections" appear. Lights indicate an arriving car. Muffled arguing can be heard. Car door slams. Sarah enters from stage left.

SARAH: What the fuck is wrong with you, Sam? Over and over again we waste money, time, and effort on this shit.

Sam enters from stage right, following Sarah.

SAM: I'm just trying to fix our relationship. Therapy helps things. Helps solve problems.

Sarah immediately snaps back.

SARAH: How's that working out? Therapy doesn't make you any less of a dick.

SAM: I'm the calm one here. I'm just trying to find a solution.

SARAH: You're calm until you don't get your way.

Sam chuckles.

SAM: Is it me or you throwing the tantrum? Like a *child*.

Sarah snaps, throwing a glass towards Sam. It smashes on the wall, missing him.

SARAH: You vicious shit!

Sam loses his temper. He charges her and grabs her by the collar while he raises his voice.

SAM: This is exactly why we need therapy Sarah! You're out of control! Get the fuck upstairs and change. We're going to be late.

Sarah stares at him, filled with anger.

SARAH: Why do I need to change?

SAM: *(Walking away)* You're in your fucking sweats.

SARAH: So?

SAM: So, my fuck- can we not look good for our therapist? He already thinks we're two fucking psych patients. Which ain't far off from you.

SARAH: Excuse me? What! What did you call me?

SAM: A psych patient. You belong in a psych ward.

SARAH: Me? Me? You're two steps away from Chris Browning me.

Sam fake laughs.

SAM: Go fuck yourself.

Sarah screams in frustration.

SARAH: Why can't you listen to me! I don't want to go!

Sam pauses for a second.

SAM: You finished?

SARAH: You fucker.

SAM: Our appointment is in half an hour. We need to get going.

SARAH: Just go ahead, dismiss my feelings yet again. Every time I raise a concern with you, you just brush it off.

SAM: If you feel that strongly about it, then we can talk. In the therapy session.

SARAH: I don't want to go!

SAM: Get in the fucking car! It's one hundred quid a session!

SARAH: *(Mocking him)* Hundred quid a session. Typical Sam. Only thing you fucking talk about is money. Oh! I provide! I do all this! All that! All for you! Go fuck yourself. And your money.

Sam chuckles.

SAM: So, fucking grateful.

SARAH: What have I to be grateful for when I'm stuck with you.

Sam's agitation visibly grows. He walks to the door and violently opens it.

SAM: There's the door! Wide open! Why don't you walk on out you miserable bitch.

A beat.

But no. No, you won't go. You need me.

Sarah laughs at him.

SARAH: Because why? Hm? You pay for my home, university bills, car.

SAM: *(Scoffs)* I'm the one with the job. What do you do? Sit around all day, go to one or two lectures a week? I dropped out of university so I can provide for you, so we can make a family.

SARAH: My fucking point.

Pause.

I didn't make that choice for you Sam, don't throw it my face.

SAM: So, what? You'd rather I didn't propose?

SARAH: I didn't say that.

SAM: So, what are you saying, then?

Sarah lets out a long sigh. She tries to calm herself down.

SARAH: I'm grateful for you getting a job and providing for us. You know that. I've said that before. But you must realise that it's not just an opportunity for you, it's an opportunity for both of us.

Sam sits down.

SAM: It just feels one-sided. I'm tired of it.

SARAH: Oh, come on Sam.

SAM: It does, I mean you don't even ask how I am anymore, you don't even say good morning, or that you love me.

SARAH: I say it all the time!

SAM: You say it back, there's a difference.

He pauses. Sighs.

It just seems like you're not interested anymore.

There is a silence.

SARAH: If I wasn't interested I wouldn't have got back with you.

SAM: You've said before, you only got back with me because you saw how it affected me and how I basically begged for you to come back.

SARAH: That's not the full story. I was affected too.

SAM: Really? You didn't seem phased. You just went about your life normally.

Sarah snaps back.

SARAH: That's not fair. I had a lot going on. You know what, Sam. I have a lot going on right now too. So, sorry if I don't have time to smother you and be all over you. I'm not like that. If you want that you can fuck off to the next slag who wants you.

SAM: Jesus, Sarah. I don't want to argue again.

Sarah laughs.

SARAH: You cause the arguments! You're the centre of all the shit in the relationship!

SAM: *(With sarcasm)* Yeah okay that's fine, blame it all on me.

SARAH: But you are! You start all the fights!

SAM: Sarah, stop. Stop it please. Please. Just get in the car. Don't change. Look like that, I don't give a fuck. But please. I don't want to lose another deposit.

There is a pause. Sarah looks at Sam. She is furious. She scoffs and exits, nudging into him as she leaves. Sam scratches his head. The lights dim. Scene ends.

Scene two

The stage is bare. We hear a voiceover of Sam.

SAM: I don't love Sarah. She's toxic. Manipulative. Aggressive. Too much.

A beat.

Or so I've been told. In reality. I love Sarah. I love her more than anything.

Suddenly. Sam appears on stage right. A spotlight shines upon him. Music serenades him. A montage of him and Sarah appears on the cyclorama.

She's incredibly intelligent, yet she doesn't quite know it. She loves the strangest foods and has an odd – but unique sense of taste. She loves her family. She takes care of her brother in a way that anyone would admire and respect. She cares for others, no matter who it could be - she's just wired that way.

A pause. Moments of Sarah laughing with a family onto the screen.

She's an incredible cook. All the meals she's made me I've eaten every bite, she's sensational.

Montage of Sam and Sarah cooking and laughing together, projected onto the cyclorama.

She has a unique and yet beautiful music taste for someone her age. She's just like her mother in that way. It's very sweet, I envy the relationship that they share. It's rare.

Homing in on a video of Sarah and her mother joking and laughing together.

I love that she claims she's not affectionate, but she would be the first one to comfort me after a bad day.

Sarah and Sam embracing on the screen.

She's brave and courageous. She's a risk taker, and not afraid of a good challenge. She's an amazing dancer, it makes me jealous. I wish I could dance as good as her - it's infectious I mean it really is, she can make you get up and dance no matter what mood you're in. Not to mention that singing. I mean you just have to hear it.

Video of Sarah and Sam dancing.

She doesn't give into my moods, whether I'm screaming the house down, or hysterically crying. She doesn't judge. She understands and she-

A beat.

She listens.

Montage on the screen fades. The lights focus in on Sam. He swallows. He has a more serious tone in his voice.

I mean I'm not sure how she feels for me, she doesn't make it clear. But. I love her company. She makes me feel safe.

He pauses. Sam addresses the audience.

That's something that's very rare for me.

Sam exits. Sarah enters the stage; the montage begins again on the cyclorama.

SARAH: Sam is a very gentle person; he takes people's feelings into consideration – sometimes too much. He's incredibly hard working, and he has this face he pulls when he's really concentrating on something. Which has always made me smile.

Video of Sam, smiling and interacting with people.

He's naturally intelligent, I mean I could study for a test for months and Sam would pick up a book the night before and do better, he's just gifted that way.

Sam. Studying late at night projected onto the screen.

He's got incredible style and he always manages to look good in unflattering situations, and that's hard - especially for a man. He's great with children and with my younger brother, sometimes I think he visits for him instead of me.

Montage of Sam, laughing with Sarah's younger brother.

He always insists on paying for meals when we're on dates, even when he has no money. I've always found that quite charming but also idiotic. He's got an infectious smile and he's incredibly funny, his jokes are always so perfectly timed.

Sam and Sarah sitting at a restaurant. Sam pulls out his credit card. Sarah laughs and directs him to put it away.

He's a picky eater, a strange eater, I mean he won't eat a simple sandwich, but he can put away chicken five days a week. I've never seen it before it's incredible.

Sarah cooking. Sam walks in with a takeaway. He laughs.

He can remember all the inside jokes, and always records you doing stupid shit on a night out. He uses it against you the next morning. It's, quite sick actually.

Video of Sarah laughing, drunk. Sam records her on his phone. They both laugh.

Most importantly. He showed me kindness and affection when I needed it the most. He was the first boy to really, consistently, love me for me. Check up on me, compliment me and genuinely mean it. He loved me.

Sam holding Sarah. He brushes her hair and kisses her on the forehead.

He's up front about his feelings and he communicates them, well – to the best of his ability. He makes it known that he loves me.

Sarah and Sam join. They sit in Doctor Adams' office. There are three chairs placed along the stage. Sarah and Sam ruffle their pages.

DOCTOR ADAMS: That was lovely, Sarah. Thank you.

Sam coughs.

SARAH: Jesus Christ, what's the problem now?

Sam laughs.

SAM: I coughed, Sarah. Doesn't mean there's a problem.

SARAH: No, Sam. You're being disrespectful. I'm being vulnerable.

SAM: You're bullshitting really. Is what you're doing.

Sarah grows irritated.

SARAH: Of course, I'm bullshitting. You wouldn't even know. You don't listen to a word that I say.

SAM: You grow tired of it after a while, Sarah.

SARAH: What's that supposed to mean.

Sam responds with passive aggression.

SAM: Whatever you think it means.

Sarah's blood boils.

SARAH: You cunt!

Sarah stands up. Doctor Adams intervenes.

DOCTOR ADAMS: Okay! Okay! Why don't we all just calm down please.

There is a pause in the room.

All this aggression. Pettiness between the two of you. It's the central problem of your relationship.

Sarah laughs.

SARAH: Pettiness?

SAM: Just sit down.

Sarah snaps. She points at Sam.

SARAH: Don't tell me what to fucking do!

DOCTOR ADAMS: This is exactly what I was talking about.

She turns to Sarah.

Now, sit down please.

SAM: Do what the doctor says.

Sarah reluctantly sits down. She is furious with Sam.

SARAH: I can't sit in a room with him.

DOCTOR ADAMS: Why's that?

SARAH: Him! Look at him!

Sam laughs.

Look at his face! Smug fuck.

Sam laughs again.

SAM: Smug? You think I'm happy with a relationship like this? Why do you think I'm here?

SARAH: You want to see me lose.

SAM: You've got a victim complex, that's what it is. Poor, fucking Sarah.

SARAH: You constantly belittle me.

SAM: No. You want that to be the case. You manipulate a situation for *your* benefit. Your gain. That's what it is.

SARAH: You think I want to be belittled?

Sam pauses. He pretends to think.

SAM: Yes.

SARAH: Prick.

Doctor Adams tries to stop the pair.

DOCTOR ADAMS: Okay. Maybe we shou-

SARAH: You never listen.

Sam chuckles.

SAM: You're repeating yourself.

SARAH: I'm repeating myself because you didn't listen the first time!

Sam ignores her. He addresses Doctor Adams with sarcasm.

SAM: Got a fucking broken record over here.

DOCTOR ADAMS: Sam, please.

SARAH: You see the shit I have to deal with, here?

DOCTOR ADAMS: Sarah.

SARAH: The fuck did I do?

DOCTOR ADAMS: Calm. Down. I won't say it again. If you continue like this, you're going to have to leave.

   Sam whispers under his breath.

SAM: Jesus.

   Sarah stops. She breathes slowly.

DOCTOR ADAMS: I appreciate this is a sensitive topic for the both of you. You both are clearly in an agitated state. Maybe we can continue this another time. A time when you both are calmer.

SAM: Another session wasted.

   Tears roll down Sarah's face. She looks at Sam.

SARAH: Fuck you.

DOCTOR ADAMS: Sarah. Please. Now is no time for strong words.

SARAH: So, you're going to take his side?

SAM: There's no sides.

DOCTOR ADAMS: Precisely.

SARAH: Jesus Christ.

Sarah places her hands on her head.

SAM: What's wrong now?

SARAH: No one's believing me.

DOCTOR ADAMS: Sarah.

SARAH: No one's listening to my side.

DOCTOR ADAMS: There's no sides Sarah. Again, there's just people trying to help each other. However, you both aren't communicating the right way.

Sarah loses her temper. She stands up.

SARAH: Except there is! There's my side. The truth! Then there's his. His bullshit spun up lies to make me look bad!

Sam sighs. Shaking his head.

SAM: *(Muttering)* What the fuck.

DOCTOR ADAMS: Sarah. Calm down, please.

SARAH: No. Fuck this.

Sarah walks towards the door.

I'm leaving. You two are welcome to suck each other's dicks while I'm gone.

Sarah storms out the room, slamming the door as she leaves. The silence of the room is deafening. Sam and Doctor Adams are left alone. Sam clears his throat.

SAM: I'm sorry, doc.

Doctor Adams fails to reply.

This shit's hard. All this.

There is more silence.

DOCTOR ADAMS: Would you like to talk about it?

SAM: Talk about myself?

DOCTOR ADAMS: Well, you might as well. We've time left in the session.

Sam sighs.

SAM: Okay.

He clears his throat.

It's tiring. Being at each other's throats. All the time. I'm what? Twenty-one? I'm young, and I'm tired. Tired repeating the same day over and over again.

DOCTOR ADAMS: What do you mean by that? The same day. Over and over again?

Sam sighs, again.

SAM: Yeah. It's like. Wake up. Argue. Go to work. Deal with pricks. Go home. Deal with a bigger prick, about something only a prick would worry about.

DOCTOR ADAMS: What are you saying Sam?

SAM: She's a prick. I'm tired dealing with a childish prick every day.

DOCTOR ADAMS: Then leave.

Sam is shocked.

SAM: S-Sorry?

DOCTOR ADAMS: Leave the relationship.

There is silence.

From what I see, it's unhealthy. From what you tell me you're unhappy.

SAM: I've never thought about it like that.

DOCTOR ADAMS: Maybe think about it. Are you even happy anymore? Is Sarah happy anymore?

SAM: I don't know. I really don't know.

Scene ends.

Scene three

The lights brighten on a coffee shop in the local town, Sarah and Annie enter, carrying bags of shopping.

ANNIE: You don't have to say much. But, what happened with you and Sam in the session?

SARAH: I don't know. It's pointless. It doesn't work – we keep on fighting over nothing. I tried to explain to him it's a waste of our time, but he wasn't for listening.

ANNIE: *(Scoffs)* Dick. Well, I don't think you should get too worked up about it. He might just be scared that there's no progress, and then he takes it out on you.

Sarah sighs.

SARAH: But that's not fair though, is it?

ANNIE: Well, no. But I'm not justifying what he did. He really does love you, and he doesn't want to lose you. And after all that's happened. I think it's just playing on his mind.

SARAH: I'm just sick of his bullshit. It's so repetitive and exhausting. He just blows up, causes a scene, storms off, then he comes back at the end of the day and apologises. We're constantly moving in circles. He's driving me mad.

ANNIE: Have you said this to him?

SARAH: *(Sighs)* No. I can't get a word in. Every time we fight I just find myself throwing everything that could hurt him right at him. We don't get anywhere.

ANNIE: What do you even do in the therapy?

SARAH: Nothing. The doctor's a complete wanker. All she tells us is to communicate and 'show our feelings'. Like that's what we've been doing for the past year, you dick.

Annie laughs, Sarah laughs back.

ANNIE: Do you want to go find a seat and I'll order?

SARAH: Yeah sure. Oh! Can I have a gingerbread latte please? If they're in.

Annie nods and smiles, Sarah goes to find a seat and she bumps into Luke, an attractive young man in his twenties.

SARAH: *(Surprised)* Oh my God, Luke?

LUKE: *(Chuckling)* The one and only. How've you been, it's good to see you.

SARAH: Yeah, I'm doing good. Me and Annie are just here for a coffee, do you want to join us?

LUKE: Well, of course. I'd love to.

Sarah and Luke sit down at a table to stage right.

SARAH: You haven't met Annie, have you?

LUKE: No, I haven't. I'm excited.

They both laugh.

Um, I-I heard about you and Sam breaking up. Are you okay? How have you been coping with it all?

Sarah is taken aback.

SARAH: Oh. Um. Well, me and Sam are fine. That only lasted a couple of days. How do you know? I thought we kept it pretty well hidden.

LUKE: Oh, well John told me. He said it was rough and you guys had been rocky for a while. What happened?

SARAH: *(Stuttering)* I-I um, I. Sorry, Luke. Do you mind if we don't talk about this? It's still fresh and I'd rather move on.

Suddenly, Luke's whole demeanour changes. He acts if he is somewhat offended.

LUKE: Oh. Okay sure, I didn't know you felt so touchy about it.

Sarah laughs it off, Annie approaches the table with two coffees.

ANNIE: Hey, here you go. *(Surprised)* Oh! Luke! Lovely to meet you.

Luke stands up and Annie hugs him.

I'm Annie. I've heard a lot about you.

LUKE: *(Chuckles)* Nothing bad, I hope!

ANNIE: Oh, God no! Great things, Luke. Great things.

They all laugh.

SARAH: So, Luke. Are you still coaching that running thing?

LUKE: Yeah. Every Wednesday. You should come back. I mean you were great every week, and everyone misses you.

Annie nudges Sarah.

SARAH: Yeah, well I loved it I really did. It's just with going back to university and everything, and with Sam and his new job. It all got a bit too hectic to fit in, you know.

ANNIE: You should go back; you need a hobby. Sam will understand.

LUKE: You're more than welcome, Sarah.

SARAH: Yeah, well. Maybe.

LUKE: What's Sam's new job again? John told me he got some new fancy job, but I never heard what it was.

SARAH: *(Smiling)* He sells Porsches.

LUKE: Oh, wow. My dad has a Porsche, you know. Cracking cars.

ANNIE: Wow, maybe Sam sold him his.

They all laugh.

LUKE: No, no. My dad's had his for years. Besides, he's a tough man to sell to. Only buys from the top men.

Luke chuckles to himself. Sarah pressures Luke.

SARAH: What? What's that supposed to mean?

LUKE: Oh, no. Sorry I didn't mean to offend you.

SARAH: But what'd you mean by that?

ANNIE: Sarah, I'm sure it's nothing okay. Luke didn't mean anything by it. It's nothing against Sam.

LUKE: Yeah, no. I didn't mean anything against you, or Sam. My father just likes to purchase cars from experienced workers, that's all.

SARAH: But Sam's a good salesman. He's great at his job.

LUKE: I don't mean it like that, at all. I promise. I'm sorry I didn't mean to offend you. It was a stupid thing to bring up.

ANNIE: *(To Sarah)* Let's just leave it, yeah?

SARAH: Yeah, I'm sorry Luke. It was just a misunderstanding.

LUKE: Completely. Look, I'm sorry I have to run, I'm meeting a friend in a bit. But it was great to catch up with you Sarah, and lovely to meet you Annie.

Luke stands up and begins to leave.

SARAH: Oh, no. Don't leave on my account. Genuinely, Luke it was a misunderstanding.

LUKE: Yeah, I know. It's okay. I genuinely must go, lovely seeing you guys. I'll see you later.

Luke waves, then exits.

SARAH: Shit, you don't think he's pissed at me. Do you?

ANNIE: No, no. But what was that about?

SARAH: What do you mean? He was definitely having a dig at Sam.

ANNIE: Yeah, well. I don't know. Maybe. *(She pauses)* So fit though.

They both laugh.

SARAH: Annie!

ANNIE: What? Don't deny it.

SARAH: It doesn't give him the right to diss my fiancé in front of me.

ANNIE: Yeah, fair enough.

SARAH: He knows about me and Sam's breakup. Like, that's so weird. Right?

ANNIE: *(Surprised)* What? Really? How?

SARAH: Apparently John told him. He wouldn't do that to Sam though, would he?

ANNIE: I wouldn't be surprised.

SARAH: Yeah. He's quite the shit mixer. Sam told him we broke up, and suddenly my whole university class knew, and I don't even know half of them.

ANNIE: The man can cause shit, whether he means to or not.

SARAH: I don't get it. The number of times he's let Sam down is unforgiveable in my book. Sam lets him away with far too much. He was the first person to spread word of our breakup, Sam and I said to him to not say anything. The number of times I've told Sam to just drop him, he goes all, "Oh, well he's my best mate. I don't mind. I don't have anyone else. You've got Annie, you've got your family". Like, I'm sorry but, how's that my fault?

ANNIE: I feel bad for him, there's not really any winning for him in these situations.

SARAH: What do you mean?

ANNIE: He hasn't got many people to talk to. The only person he has to talk to is your councillor, and I shouldn't even know that information. John told me. I was surprised you didn't tell me.

SARAH: It's not my place to tell. *(Sighs)* I think I need to speak to Sam.

ANNIE: I don't know, give him some space for a while, go back home for the day. See your family.

SARAH: Yeah, I've missed them so much.

She chuckles.

ANNIE: Yeah. What's the time anyway? When's the next bus?

SARAH: Oh, here. I don't know actually. *(Looking at her phone)* Shit! We're going to miss the last one!

ANNIE: *(Standing up)* Shit!

They both get up and start giggling.

SARAH: *(Laughing)* We're such dicks!

Sarah and Annie run off stage while giggling, the lights dim to blackout, scene ends.

Scene four

In the kitchen of Sarah's family home, Sarah's father, Todd, a kind gentle man in his fifties is preparing dinner on stage right. Sarah's mother, Fiona, a youthful looking warm woman in her fifties is sitting at the dining table on stage left. Sarah's younger brother, Nathan, a kind, gentle young toddler is sitting at the dining table with Fiona. Sarah enters, holding bags of shopping and enters through the door placed upstage centre, the whole family is surprised and delighted to see her.

SARAH: Hello?

TODD: *(Surprised)* Awk! Sarah, love. We weren't expecting to see you. Come in, baby.

NATHAN: *(Smiling)* Sarah!

FIONA: *(Approaching Sarah and embracing her)* Oh, darling how wonderful it is to see you. Are you okay?

SARAH: Yeah, yeah. I'm doing good, mummy.

FIONA: Oh, lovely. Lovely.

Fiona holds Sarah's arm.

TODD: *(To Sarah)* Are you staying for your dinner?

SARAH: Y-Yeah, is that okay?

TODD: More than okay.

SARAH: *(To Nathan)* Oh! I missed you! You're so big! Come give me a hug!

NATHAN: Sarah!

Nathan runs to Sarah and gives her a hug.

FIONA: Are you staying home, love? Are you and Sam in trouble?

SARAH: Mummy, don't get me started.

FIONA: Oh, for god's sake. You two are always at each other's throats. You're not even married yet.

She chuckles.

TODD: Aye, you'll be in for a treat then Sarah.

SARAH: Oh, lovely. Can't wait.

FIONA: Awk, love. Put those bags down. Come on, sit down. You look like you've had a day of it. *(To Todd)* Todd, would you help her with those bags?

Todd takes Sarah's bags and carries them off stage, Sarah sits down at the dining table.

So, what happened now?

SARAH: Awk, no. The usual. I was just telling him how the therapy's a waste of time - and it is mummy. We've been going for weeks and there's been no solution given.

FIONA: Relationships aren't black and white, darling. You should know that by now.

SARAH: I know, but. There's zero change. Surely, we should be seeing progress.

FIONA: Tell me about it. I've been married thirty years to your father.

TODD: *(Offstage)* Oh, I heard that.

FIONA: I know you did, always ear wigging so he is. But you'll be fine sweetheart. Just give each other some breathing room. It's normal to have these teething moments when you've just moved in.

Sarah nods her head to agree.

And it doesn't help if you're engaged. All that pressure. It adds up.

SARAH: Mummy, we've been living together for three months. The teething process shouldn't last that long.

Todd re-enters.

TODD: It never ends.

FIONA: Right, you! Calm it down! *(To Sarah)* He's got a point though. Bickering is just all part of it. Unless you're unhappy ?

SARAH: Well, I don't know. I do understand that all couples bicker. It's just continuous. Repetitive.

FIONA: Hm. You know I love Sam, Sarah. But your happiness is far more important to me. If you are unhappy, maybe you should give the whole thing a reconsider? Maybe, even just hold off the engagement? Just until things calm down.

SARAH: I might do. I've been thinking about it.

FIONA: That could be the right thing for you.

Sarah nods. There is silence for a moment. Sarah clears her throat.

SARAH: I met Luke today.

FIONA: Awk, did you? Now, he's a charming boy.

SARAH: He is.

FIONA: You're not thinking about jumping ship, are you? Sarah, that's not right.

SARAH: No, mummy. No. *(She pauses)* Christ, I've thought about it before, in summer. But that's gone now. Me and Sam got through that.

FIONA: Just, don't be having too many men in your life. That never ends well.

TODD: *(To Sarah)* The only man you should have in your life is me. I'll cause you no harm.

SARAH: You cause plenty of harm, daddy.

TODD: Oh, is that right? How much harm is it to tell you your dinner is ready?

FIONA: Depends on what you're making.

They all laugh, Todd plates everyone up their dinner and sits with them at the dining table, they all begin to eat.

SARAH: It's really lovely to be home, honestly.

TODD: It's lovely to have you home. It's quiet without you. It's weird not being woken up by my lovely daughter at seven in the morning to take her to university.

SARAH: Funny one, Todd.

TODD: *(Chuckling)* Never appreciated a sleep in so much!

FIONA: *(Hits Todd)* Todd!

TODD: *(Still chuckling, to Fiona)* Sorry, love. You know I can't help myself. But we do miss you. Seriously.

SARAH: I know, I miss you too, daddy. I miss you, mummy. I miss Nathan and Jason. I really miss it here.

FIONA: You can always come back. You've got our support. Always. Are you not happy living with Sam?

SARAH: No, I am. It's not that. I-I don't know. Sometimes... *(She pauses)* Sometimes I feel like I can't breathe. You know? I need my space.

> *Todd and Fiona look at each other, concerned. Todd sighs.*

TODD: Sarah. Maybe you and Sam need some space. Proper space. Living apart from each other space.

SARAH: Really?

FIONA: Yes, baby.

TODD: We love Sam, I honestly wish the best for you. I hope it really works out between you two. I'd love him as a son in law. But Sarah. Your happiness needs to come first.

SARAH: *(Starting to tear up)* That's what mummy said.

> *Fiona holds Sarah's arm.*

FIONA: It's okay, baby.

SARAH: I-I can't just leave him. I love him. He's a piece of shit, but I love him.

TODD: Okay. You need time. Just to figure out what you want.

SARAH: I want Sam.

TODD: I know. But look at you. You're not happy, darling. Just a break is all you might need.

FIONA: Sarah, listen to me okay? What you've told me tells me that you're not happy. You and Sam might just be stuck in a rut right now. Maybe just a bit of time apart might help. Not just sleeping on the sofa. Moving out for a week or two. Serious time apart.

TODD: Distance makes the heart grow fonder.

FIONA: *(Frustrated, to Todd)* Todd.

TODD: Sorry.

FIONA: *(To Sarah)* Do you get what I'm saying?

SARAH: *(Sobbing)* Yeah.

FIONA: Do you want to give him a wee ring? Talk to him, see where the land lies?

SARAH: *(Sighs)* Yeah.

> *Sarah stands up and walks to the kitchen, she gets her phone out and dials it, lights on Todd, Fiona, and Nathan fade to black.*

Hello?

> *Lights fade on Sam, beside Sarah. He is not physically there, but on the phone to her.*

SAM: Hi, are you okay? What's up? Why are you crying?

SARAH: What do you think, Sam?

SAM: Yeah, okay. Sorry. *(He pauses)* Where are you?

SARAH: My parents. Where are you?

SAM: The flat. Come home. We have to talk.

SARAH: *(Starting to tear up again)* Sam.

SAM: What?

SARAH: I'm not coming home, tonight.

SAM: What? Why not? It's fine. It's just another fight. We always do this, come on Sarah.

SARAH: That's exactly the reason, Sam. It's constant. I just can't live in that environment anymore.

SAM: Sarah, come on. Don't be a dick.

SARAH: I think we need space for a bit.

SAM: What? I don't get it. What do you mean. A break?

SARAH: Yeah. For a week or two. Serious space.

SAM: Are you breaking up with me again?

SARAH: I can't do it. I need space. Not forever. For now. I'll come get my stuff in the morning when you're at work.

SAM: Oh. Right. Okay.

SARAH: Okay?

SAM: *(Holding back tears)* Yeah. Yeah, of course. If that's what you need.

SARAH: Okay.

There is a silence.

SAM: Do you think we should be with each other?

SARAH: What? Why do you say that?

SAM: Just answer the question.

SARAH: We just need space. Don't be like this.

SAM: Okay. Okay.

SARAH: Goodbye Sam.

He pauses. He thinks. He looks at Sarah.

SAM: Goodbye, Sarah.

Scene ends.

Act Two

Scene one

Blackout, we hear a narration of Sam's voice.

SAM: Sometimes I reminisce on the day I asked Sarah to be my girlfriend.

There is a spotlight on Sam, he is situated on slightly left to stage centre. He speaks to the audience.

It was a bitterly cold winter day. Me and Sarah had an exam in school, I believe it was a maths exam.

Sarah appears on the cyclorama screen sitting on a chair at a single wooden desk, she is writing on an exam paper and shivering.

We went into town after the exam to go Christmas shopping, and to meet a couple friends. It was a wonderful day. Very festive and very sweet.

Sam and Sarah are walking while linking arms, giggling with each other.

We met up with some friends, we got our signature gingerbread latte in our favourite coffee shop. We got lunch in our favourite restaurant. We went to our favourite shops together.

Sam and Sarah are now sitting at a table opposite each other, eating, drinking, and smiling. The lights fade. The lights brighten on Doctor Adams sitting down. Facing Sam.

I was so happy. We were so happy. I don't understand how we went from that. To where we are now.

DOCTOR ADAMS: It's tricky. There's circumstance. Things that have happened, maybe got in the way of your happiness together.

Sam thinks. He pauses for a moment.

SAM: My mother passed away. Suddenly. Fights got more frequent, and I got angry. I got bitter. I guess I took out all my grief, anger, and frustration on her.

DOCTOR ADAMS: Sarah was aware of your circumstance? She knew you were grieving.

SAM: Yeah. She tried to help.

A beat.

I regret treating Sarah the way I did. I couldn't understand my emotions. I still don't. I was just trying to get a grasp on things.

Another pause. Doctor Adams writes on a notepad.

Summer came, and me and Sarah signed up for a running club to try and break up all the fighting. Her dad gave it to her as a present for her birthday. I was never the biggest runner, but I thought I should be different, and supportive.

Sam stops for a minute. He sighs.

The coach, Luke, was very friendly, and Sarah took very fondly to him.

DOCTOR ADAMS: Was Sarah unfaithful to you?

SAM: I don't know. She never gave me a straight answer. She just shouted. Accused me of not trusting her.

He thinks.

But I don't know how I could. It was obviously flirtatious. Cheating or not, there should be a line of respect. I think.

A beat.

Maybe she just liked to tread along that line.

DOCTOR ADAMS: Where did your suspicions come from?

SAM: There was a rumour going round that Sarah and Luke got together while I was in Paris for business. She denied it, of course.

He rubs his forehead.

I don't think I ever really trusted Sarah after this. In my gut, I knew it was true. But she kept denying it. The more I pushed. The more we fought and the more I felt like I was losing my mind. That I was imagining the whole thing.

DOCTOR ADAMS: Did these arguments ever hit a boiling point?

Sam looks to the floor in shame.

SAM: Yeah. I think she noticed my lack of trust and that's when she dropped the bombshell. She didn't love me anymore.

DOCTOR ADAMS: Right.

She records on her notepad.

How did that make you feel, Sam?

Sam stares. He has a look of emptiness in his eyes.

SAM: I've never been the same since she said that. I can't look at her the same.

Doctor Adams nods.

She now says she didn't mean it, but. How do you not mean something like that? How do you not mean something so definitive. How does she go around day to day in our relationship. Acting like nothing happened? Like that statement doesn't change everything?

The lights darken. The scene changes as Sam is sitting down in his apartment. The doorbell rings, Sam rushes to open the door. His best friend, John enters. A tall young boy in his twenties.

JOHN: Awk, you alright? Annie told me you and Sarah have been at each other's throats again, so I thought I'd call by and see you. (*He laughs*) What's that you've got?

John points at a notepad, that Sam is holding.

SAM: Oh, nothing. Just, this thing we have to do for therapy. She made us write down how we met, and what went wrong. Sarah didn't even write it in the end, she made me look like a twat.

JOHN: (*Laughing*) Nothing new then, mate? And what went wrong in the first place?

SAM: Fucking Luke.

JOHN: Dick. Awk, cheer up mate it's alright. You and Sarah are always fighting, it'll get better.

SAM: I don't know this time, John. She's moved back in with her parents. It's fucked up.

John scoffs.

JOHN: And what? Me and Amanda moved in and out every week back in the day. I'll tell you what we'll do. We'll go down to town, get you a new bird. She can stay the night no problem. That'll teach her for throwing a fit and moving out. She's practically gifting you the opportunity.

Sam laughs.

SAM: And why'd you and Amanda break up again?

John thinks.

JOHN: Well. I cheated on her.

Sam laughs.

SAM: Well, that explains it. Here, sit down. Do you fancy a drink?

JOHN: Aye, a beer wouldn't go a miss. Cheers.

Sam walks over to the fridge on stage left, he grabs two beers and hands one to John.

Thanks mate.

SAM: So, what have you been up to? When are you going skiing?

JOHN: *(Drinking)* January. It'll be good fun. Just can't wait to get away from my mum to be honest with you.

SAM: You're away with Amanda aren't you?

JOHN: Aye, yeah.

SAM: Well, that's good. You really liked her, didn't you?

JOHN: She's fit like. Had a massive glow up it's unreal. Have you seen her?

Sam laughs at John.

SAM: Yeah, yeah. She's looking great.

He pauses.

So, what's wrong with your mum?

JOHN: Jesus Christ. Well. You know I never wanted to go to university right? Waste of time you know.

Sam nods.

Well, if I was going to university I said I'd study business management. It's just more me. But no, my mother said to study finance. Fucking finance! I said to her business management would be easier and I would get a better grade. No, but my mother thinks she knows better and says it's a better qualification. It might be. But I'll fuck it up and I warned her of this. So, fast forward a couple years and now I'm at my finals. Failed them didn't I. So, I've got to do an extra year. Or do another three years for business management.

SAM: Well, what did you do?

JOHN: Took the three years for business management.

SAM: Fucking hell, John! You'll be in university in your mid-twenties.

They both laugh.

JOHN: Aye, it's alright. It's fun. Shame you got sucked into the domestic life so soon mate. University life is unreal. All the clubbing and drinking. The girls. Cloud nine, brother. Cloud nine.

SAM: Yeah, well I was never really into all of that stuff. University doesn't provide a salary though, does it?

JOHN: The girls, Sam. The girls.

SAM: *(Laughing)* You are so grim, mate.

John laughs with him.

JOHN: Look, Tony wants to meet at the pub at six. You want to come? It'll be a laugh like. Cheer you up and that.

SAM: Yeah, why not? No one to go home to.

JOHN: Yes! You need to utilise this time! Go out, get drunk. Best fucking nights of your life.

SAM: Well. I wouldn't go that far. It'll be nice to catch up with Tony though. Haven't seen him in a while, and if anyone can provide good relationship advice, it's him.

JOHN: You dissing my fantastic advice?

SAM: *(Laughing)* I'd never, John. It's just Tony's played the field since he was born. He's been through every situation according to man.

JOHN: That is very true.

SAM: Should we head on then?

JOHN: Aye, time to get shit faced. Let's go.

Sam and John get up and put on their jackets/coats. They leave from stage right, there is now blackout. Scene ends.

Scene two

In the local pub, Sam and John enter from stage left. T They meet their friends Ryan and Tony. Ryan, a young man in his twenties with long curly hair and a beanie. He is a mutual friend of Sam and John. Tony, Sam's long-time friend is a young man in his twenties, he is tall with short black hair. Tony and Ryan cheer and greet Sam and John as they enter.

TONY: Boys! Long-time no see!

Tony hugs John.

Sam! I've missed you so much, man!

Tony hugs Sam.

SAM: My brother. Missed you. It's so good to see you.

RYAN: *(Drunkenly)* Motherfuckers! I love you both! How are you!

Ryan hugs Sam and John.

Round on me! Round on me!

They all cheer.

TONY: So, what have you boys been up to?

SAM: Well, John has signed himself up for another three years of university.

TONY: Fuck off!

  Tony laughs.

JOHN: Game's the game, isn't it.

TONY: Jesus, John. You won't be out of there until your mid-twenties. At least.

  Sam points at Tony.

SAM: Exactly what I said.

JOHN: Piss off, the lot of you. In five years. I'll be making a fortune. That's what my mum says.

SAM: You'll still be there in five years, John!

  They all laugh.

JOHN: Laugh it up, laugh it up.

TONY: We are, John.

  Ryan enters from stage right, carrying four drinks.

RYAN: Here we are, lads. Here we are. Drinks on me. We are getting fucked tonight, that's for sure.

TONY: Jesus, Ryan! Did you order us straight whiskey? Who do you think we are for fucks sake! Those old men over there!

RYAN: Boys, you have not lived until you've had a night out like me.

JOHN: Sounds like a plan to me.

SAM: You couldn't have got a mixer, no?

RYAN: The fuck's a mixer?

SAM: Right.

Sam and Tony laugh.

JOHN: I'm down for this shit.

John drinks the whiskey and immediately starts coughing. Tony, Sam, and Ryan laugh.

SAM: Nice one, John.

TONY: *(Laughing)* Jesus, John.

JOHN: Right, to change the subject. Tony, what's all this I hear about you and Ruby. Fighting again?

TONY: Oh, you know us two. Always fighting and shit. She's just overreacting.

SAM: What was it this time?

TONY: Well, you know my ex, Daisy?

JOHN: Unfortunately.

They all laugh.

TONY: Well, you see on Halloween Ruby asked me to spend the night at her house. Carve pumpkins and do all that wholesome shit.

They all nod and agree.

RYAN: Well, who'd want to do that?

TONY: Aye, exactly. Well, Daisy invited me to go out with her mates in a field near her house. Put some shit on fire and drink and that. You know, something more Halloween themed.

They laugh.

SAM: Yes, burning shit in a field with your ex, screams Halloween more than carving pumpkins with your actual girlfriend.

TONY: Aye, yes! Well, I thought I wouldn't tell Ruby about it and say my family are doing something for Halloween, like a family party or something. But then she was asking why she couldn't come.

JOHN: What did you say to that?

TONY: Oh, I just told her they don't like her.

They all laugh.

SAM: You must be joking. No wonder she was pissed off! You lied to her saying you were going to see your family to get out of seeing her. But then you actually went to see your ex-girlfriend. And to top it off you told her your family doesn't like her!

They laugh again.

JOHN: Brutal.

TONY: Just how it is.

SAM: So, where's she now then.

TONY: Sure, her and your Sarah and all their mates are going clubbing tonight. Didn't you know?

Sam looks at John, shocked and confused. He pulls himself together.

SAM: Oh, aye yeah. I completely forgot. A lot going on in my head.

Sam laughs it off.

Where are they all going, again?

TONY: Fuck, I don't even remember the name of the place. I switch off at everything Ruby says, to be honest. Let me think.

Tony pauses.

I know it's around the corner. The place they usually go.

SAM: Oh, yeah. No, I know. I remember now.

JOHN: Boys, why aren't we out there clubbing and shit. We're sitting in here like a bunch of fifty-year-old men. It's sad.

RYAN: What are you on about? This is peak life here! Look around you!

They all stop to look around them. The atmosphere is dead with a couple of old men sitting down, drinking or playing pool if possible. There is old style slow music playing in the background.

SAM: *(With sarcasm)* You're right on the money, Ryan.

JOHN: This is tragic.

RYAN: Well, drink up! You're sitting there stone cold sober, of course it's tragic!

TONY: He makes a solid point.

JOHN: *(Standing up)* Right, I'm off for a piss. If I don't come back to at least a couple birds in here. I'm away.

John exits.

TONY: *(Laughing)* Well, he's fucking dreaming. Birds here? In the Old Bull. The give away's in the name.

SAM: That makes zero sense, Tony.

They laugh. Ryan finishes his drink.

RYAN: Another round?

TONY: Jesus, Ryan

Sam laughs.

RYAN: I'll take that as a yes then, won't I?

He gets up to go to the bar, he exits through stage right.

TONY: Fancy a smoke?

SAM: Go on, then.

TONY: Alright.

They both stand up and exit, laughing together. Scene ends.

Scene three

In the smoking area at the local pub. It is cold and empty. There are a few chairs and benches scattered upstage, with an umbrella and a picnic bench with an ash tray on it to stage left. Tony and Sam enter from stage right, laughing. Tony lights his cigarette and smokes it. He offers it to Sam, and he takes it.

TONY: It's really great to see you, Sam. Honestly.

SAM: You too. You have no idea. I've missed you. We've barely spent a day apart since primary school. We've grown up together.

TONY: *(Chuckling)* Good days, mate. They were good.

Tony laughs to himself.

Yeah, do you remember that time when were like ten, we climbed up the door of your sister's room.

Sam laughs.

SAM: Oh, fuck.

TONY: *(Laughing hysterically)* And the whole thing fucking caved in on us!

They both laugh with each other.

SAM: We were something different back then.

TONY: Aw, mate. I know.

He pauses.

You know. Is everything alright? I don't know, correct me if I'm wrong here – but. You don't seem yourself. Is something bothering you?

Sam's face drops. He lets out a sigh.

What's wrong? You can tell me anything. I'm your friend.

Sam pauses. He takes a draw from the cigarette.

SAM: Well, um. Me and. Me and Sarah aren't really on speaking terms.

A beat

She moved out.

Tony nods his head. For a moment he is speechless. He lights up another cigarette and smokes it.

TONY: I don't know if that's permanent. Me and Ruby fight all the time and she's always moving from mine to her parents, to her mates. Relationships are just complicated.

SAM: We've been fighting for a while.

A pause.

How long does this stage in a relationship last?

TONY: I'm usually out of there before that stage. But with Ruby. It's a lot, but. We make up quick. We just make it work.

SAM: Yeah, you know, we used to be like that. But ever since summer, and Luke. You know. Things changed.

TONY: Who's Luke? Where did this guy come from? She cheat on you?

SAM: No, no. At least not that I know of, anyway. She denies it completely.

Sam thinks.

They were so close, not just in a friendly way. There's a fine line you know. I'm all for giving her freedom. But there's an element of respect. Isn't there?

TONY: I agree. One hundred percent.

A beat.

Who is this guy? Where did she meet him?

Sam laughs.

SAM: Well. Her dad bought us a running club membership for over summer. I only went because I'm good mates with her dad. It was fun. Wasn't all that, but. It was fun.

A moment.

Luke was the main coach there. Funny, friendly, a good-looking guy you know?

Sam sighs.

He had a lot I didn't. They'd go for coffee dates when I was away in Paris. She'd always say how she loves 'being around him'. I suppose I was a bit.

Sam stops. He collects himself.

A bit self-conscious around him. I felt that. He. I don't know. Emasculated me, in a way.

Tony nods. He takes in what Sam has said.

TONY: I think, maybe you were just threatened by him. Or jealous? I mean, you saw her being truly happy with this guy. Laughing and smiling and getting on. Meeting up without you. Any guy would feel threatened by that, she can't pin it on you. Like you said there's a fine line between what's disrespectful and respectful. It seems like she liked to overstep that line a fair bit.

Sam thinks.

SAM: But why would she do that? That's what I don't get.

TONY: A reaction. To piss you off. Maybe to cause more problems in the relationship so a breakup wouldn't be her fault, and she can blame it on you for ruining it.

Sam pauses.

SAM: Do you think she'd do that?

Tony sighs.

TONY: I don't know. Maybe. All girls are different. But I know Sarah. She has a history of being manipulative.

SAM: Manipulative?

TONY: She just likes to twist certain situations to get her own way. She'll lie, shift the blame and whatever.

Sam is shocked.

SAM: I don't think she's like that, Tony. I know her.

TONY: Well, I'm only telling you from what I've heard. She was like that to one of my mates a while ago.

SAM: They only dated for two months. You can't really read someone that well in two months.

TONY: Well, there's a reason he left so quick. I really do think she's manipulative, Sam. Think about all those situations with your sister. She never put in an effort with her. Ever. There must be some reason for that.

SAM: She was intimidated by her.

TONY: Sam, I know your sister. Intimidating would not be the word to describe her. She's not some villain. She's very outgoing so it can't be that.

SAM: Well, what do you think then?

TONY: I don't know. But after everything your family went through. Losing your fucking mum. And she still wouldn't be civil or even speak to any of your family. Treating you the way that she does. It's messed up, Sam.

Sam pauses, he is visibly upset now. He looks up. Taking a draw from his cigarette to compose himself.

SAM: Yeah.

TONY: We could all see from the start. She was a bit controlling. She knew your sister has the most influence on you, because you look up to her so much. I don't think she liked that. Maybe she was intimidated.

Sam stares, with a blank expression on his face.

SAM: Maybe so.

Tony looks at him, confused.

TONY: What's wrong?

Sam sits down on a bench.

SAM: It just feels like years of my life was.

A beat.

A lie. Big. Fucking, manipulative lie!

Tony attempts to reassure Sam.

TONY: It's okay, Sam. It's alright. It's just my guess.

SAM: What if it's true, Tony? What do I do? My whole life is fucking ruined. I poured my entire future into this girl.

TONY: Sam. You've got us. We're never going to leave you stranded. You've got support around you, I promise. She may not be any of those things.

Tony pauses.

It's just what makes sense to me.

Sam snaps.

SAM: Do you have any other theories about my dying relationship?

Sam's anger and irritation begins to grow.

TONY: It's not like that, Sam.

Sam scoffs.

SAM: Sarah says that all the time. All the fucking time.

Sam's anger increases.

TONY: What do you mean?

SAM: *(With frustration and utter rage)* She doesn't fucking listen. She deflects every valid point back to me. Oh, 'It's not like that, Sam' and 'I didn't say that Sam', like it's all my fucking fault! Like, Jesus! Show some responsibility. Own up to your fucked up mistakes. But, no! Sarah's too proud! It's always my fault.

Sam's anger boils over.

She speaks to me like a piece of shit! You want to know something? You know she never says she loves me? She doesn't like to hold my hand in public because she says, 'I don't want people to see us like that'. What the fuck! You don't want people to see us like what?! In a romantic setting!? Together!? Oh, how humiliating! How dare Sarah be seen with me in public. It's like she's ashamed of me.

Sam laughs. Tony watches on.

She can't remember our anniversaries. She's never remembered a single one. And I! Have to play along and be like, 'Oh, I forgot too, ha-ha!' Then I have to go to my car and take back an expensive gift I got for her. You know what she wrote in my birthday card this year? She was pissed at me, on my birthday and wrote, "Hope you're not as much as an asshole next year. Maybe grow the fuck up." I've worked off my ass so she can go to university. You know how she repays me? Not showing up to classes, going out clubbing every other night! Complaining! Whining! Being a disrespectful! Fucking! Bitch!

Sam is tearing up, he pants, his heart beats fast. He pauses.

She doesn't love me! Alright! She doesn't! She admitted to it.

Sam cries.

I'm pathetic. I stayed with a woman who hates me. I've wasted my life on a woman who hates me. I hate my life. I can't do this. I can't. I fucking. Can't.

Sam falls to his knees, breaking down. Tony attempts to help him.

TONY: Sam, Sam. It's okay. It's okay buddy.

SAM: *(Screaming in pure emotion)* What the fuck! What the fuck!

Sam punches the ground, repeatedly.

Fuck! Fuck! Fuck!

Tony stands back, scared of Sam. Sam sobs.

I'm sorry.

TONY: *(Shakingly)* It's okay.

Tony approaches Sam as he sobs on the ground.

TONY: Come on mate, stand up. It's alright. I'm here for you.

Tony helps Sam stand up. Sam's hand is bloody and bruised. He continues to sob with a blank expression on his face.

SAM: I'm sorry. I'm a mess.

TONY: No mate.

SAM: I'm pathetic.

TONY: You're not. Quit talking like this.

Sam starts to sob again.

SAM: I hate myself. I hate my life.

Tony reassures Sam.

TONY: No. You're not pathetic. We're going to get through this okay, you're just stuck in a rut. This is why you have us. Your friends. Everyone gets low. You're going to get through this.

Sam looks at tony. He realises the mess he has created around him.

SAM: I'm sorry.

A beat.

I need to go. It was nice seeing you.

Sam walks off to stage right, he exits.

TONY: *(Calling after him)* Sam! Fuck.

He pauses.

What the fuck do I do now?

Tony gets his phone out his pocket and dials it. He is visibly anxious and worried for Sam's well-being, scene ends.

Scene four

In a quiet street, in the town. Sam enters from stage right. He is visibly upset as he sobs, we can hear Sarah shouting from a distance.

SARAH: *(From a distance)* Ruby! Ruby! Where are you? Are you okay? Ruby!

Sam looks around. Confused. Startled.

Ruby!

Sarah appears from stage left; she sees Sam immediately. She is shocked.

What are you doing here?

SAM: Nice to see you too.

SARAH: Oh, piss off Sam.

SAM: That's just. Lovely.

He pauses.

Why are you here?

SARAH: I'm looking for Ruby.

SAM: What happened?

SARAH: She said she was going for a smoke, but I couldn't find her in the smoking area. So, now I'm out here looking for her.

SAM: On your own?

SARAH: Yeah, well no one else wanted to come. They said she always does this.

SAM: She does.

SARAH: Well, I'm going to go look for her. Goodbye, Sam.

SAM: Sarah, no. I can't let you do that. It's dangerous. You're on your own walking in these streets at night, calling and looking for someone who clearly isn't out there.

SARAH: What the fuck do you know?!

SAM: She does this every single time she's out, Sarah. She's looking for attention. That's all.

SARAH: You're a piece of shit. You're going to put this girl's life at risk then?

SAM: Act normal for once, Sarah. No one's life is at risk. She's at home. You look like a fucking fool.

SARAH: Oh, just fuck off Sam! I'm going.

SAM: I can't let you go out there.

Sam pauses.

I love you, and I care about you. You're my priority. I have to keep you safe. I can't let you go out there. Let me call someone, what about your brother?

SARAH: Fuck off. Don't disturb him. He works long hours.

She begins to storm off.

SAM: Right. *(To himself)* Fuck.

Sam grabs his phone and rings Sarah's older brother, Jason. Sarah stops.

Jason. Hello. I'm sorry to call you but Sarah's out here walking around the streets alone looking for her friend.

He pauses, listening to Jason.

Yeah, no I agree. She's drunk. Not listening to me, that's why I'm calling you.

He pauses again while Jason answers him. Sam passes the phone to Sarah, who is staring at him. Disgusted, angry, and full of hatred.

SARAH: Jason! What the fuck! No!

She pauses while Jason speaks to her over the phone.

No, you don't understand! I'm a grown fucking woman!

A beat.

Piss off! No! I'm fine! It's all Sam's fault!

Sam is standing, alone. Listening. He feels empty. Guilty. Powerless. Sarah is now shouting down the phone, mute.

SAM: *(To himself)* Fuck.

Suddenly, Annie enters from stage left. She is looking for Sarah and sees her on the phone. She is now confused and approaches Sam.

ANNIE: *(To Sam)* What's going on? Why's she so angry?

SAM: I don't even know. She's batshit crazy.

ANNIE: Who's she on the phone to? What happened Sam?

SAM: I found her out here looking for Ruby. I tried to explain to her Ruby is completely fine, and just looking for attention.

ANNIE: Oh my god, Sam.

SAM: Well, in a few words.

ANNIE: *(Agitated)* Sam.

SAM: Well, yeah I'm sorry – but. She's fine! We all know she's fine. She's overacting as always. I don't know why you all let her do this. Call her out on it!

ANNIE: Sam.

   Annie pauses.

Ruby's bi-polar.

SAM: Annie, with all due respect. She self-diagnosed herself with it from google. Tony tried to tell her one time that he thinks he might have it, and she claimed it was 'her thing.' If you think that's real then there's no helping any of you.

ANNIE: Right, Sam. Leave it. What's going on with Sarah? She's going mental. Who's she on the phone with?

SAM: Jason.

ANNIE: Jason, her brother? Why's she on the phone screaming with Jason?

SAM: I rang him. Told him she was out here looking for Ruby on her own.

ANNIE: Jesus, Sam. Why? Leave him out, he works long hours.

SAM: I had to. She wouldn't listen to me. I can't let her go do that. Anything could happen. It's not safe.

Annie sighs.

I had her safety in mind. I have to keep her safe. That's my job, that's my priority.

ANNIE: They look like they're locked in an almighty row. She's going to hate you for this.

Sam is now silent. He stares at the ground and looks back up with a tear in his eye.

SAM: She already does. There's nothing I can do about that. I can at least try and keep her safe at the same time.

Sarah hangs up the phone, she walks towards Sam and hands in to him, aggressively.

SARAH: You've just caused a fucking fight, you know that?!

SAM: I'm sorry.

SARAH: No, but you're not! You're an overprotective twat!

Sam sighs.

SAM: Okay.

ANNIE: I'm going to go back inside, Sarah. Meet me in there soon, yeah?

SARAH: Yeah, sorry. I'll join you in a minute, Annie.

ANNIE: Alright.

Annie exits, whilst looking at Sam with concern.

SAM: I'm sorry.

SARAH: Do you even know what you've done?

SAM: I did what I had to do, Sarah. You refused to hear me out. You were being irrational.

SARAH: Who are you to decide when I'm being irrational?

SAM: Well, usually when you're drunk and start swearing. That's kind of a big indicator.

SARAH: This isn't a joke, Sam! Get real!

SAM: Oh, come off it, Sarah! I rang your fucking brother. The world's still spinning. You have no idea what could've happened if you went out there!

SARAH: You don't get to make that decision for me, Sam.

SAM: I'm trying to protect you.

SARAH: You control me.

SAM: That's pathetic, Sarah.

Sarah laughs at Sam.

SARAH: Pathetic!? You know what's pathetic?

Her anger increases, she grits her teeth as she shouts at Sam.

You. You're a pathetic excuse of a fucking man.

She laughs.

You want to protect me? No. You know half the things that hurt me are *you.* You, Sam! The most hurtful things that have been said to me have been said by you. You don't want to protect me. You want to *control* me. You're manipulative. You're a piece of shit, Sam.

Her anger boils.

I can't believe I let myself fall in love with you, I just can't. You know what. You're selfish. Everything you do is for yourself, and you know the worst part? You disguise it as you're doing it for me, or your friends. But really Sam, you do it for yourself!

Blowing up, she begins to hit Sam, repeatedly.

Fuck you! Just fuck you! No wonder everyone in your family left you!

She stops. Tears trickle down Sam's face. He is shocked and hurt.

SAM: *(Quietly, with meaning)* Fuck you.

Sarah is now panting with anger.

They're *dead.* Sarah. Most of them. You never listened to how hard that is for me.

SARAH: *(Shouting)* Sam! Everyone has dead relatives! Everyone! Take a look at the situation right now! Look at the bigger picture!

SAM: What are you talking about? What the fuck does all this have to do with the 'bigger picture'? Are you seriously saying that to me right now?

A beat.

You're fucking drunk, Sarah.

SARAH: Yeah! Yeah, I'm drunk, Sam! What's the problem!?

Sam looks at Sarah with tears in his eyes.

SAM: *(Sighing)* Okay, Sarah. Good for you.

SARAH: My tired brother is on his way anyway. Thanks. Selfish bastard.

Sam laughs. A tear falls down his face.

SAM: Alright. Let's just hope he gets here soon.

SARAH: Whatever, Sam. Why are you so annoyed? You're the one who ruined my night.

SAM: You ruined it for yourself.

SARAH: Wow! You are so self-centred it's unreal.

She pauses and thinks.

Do you know what this reminds me of?

Sam is fed up.

SAM: What's that, Sarah?

SARAH: When I graduated school. When I got my results.

A beat.

You. Made the whole day about yourself.

She laughs at Sam.

You accused me of getting with Luke!

Sam looks at his fiancé. With a cold stare.

SAM: You wanted to spend the day with him. Instead of me. He didn't even go to our school. Listen to yourself it wasn't *your* graduation. It was *ours*. Our day. Our results. It was mine too.

He laughs to himself.

You're so unbelievably selfish.

SARAH: Oh, shut the fuck up. Please! You're the one who called me a slag for spending time with Luke!

Sam snaps.

SAM: Can you blame me! Can you actually blame me, Sarah?

A moment of silence.

SARAH: *(Shocked)* Oh my god, Sam. Are you seriously standing by what you said and did that day?

Sarah laughs at Sam.

After all the apologising and all the tears, you're seriously standing here and telling me that you stand by it? Sam, you made it all about you. I have never been hurt by someone more than when you said that to me, and I found myself comforting you because you felt –

what? Guilty? Sorry for yourself? I was the one who was hurt, Sam.

SAM: Go fuck yourself.

SARAH: You're so - manipulative! Fuck you!

Jason enters, worried.

JASON: Sarah? Sam? What's going on?

SAM: Yeah, I'm sorry man. I'm sorry. I just couldn't risk anything happening.

JASON: No, Sam. Thank you. You did the right thing. Are you okay to get home?

Sam thinks.

SAM: I. Um. Yeah, no I'll be fine. Thanks.

JASON: Alright, mate. Thanks again.

Sam nods.

SAM: Yeah.

SARAH: *(To Jason)* Can we go now?

JASON: Yeah, yeah. Come on. See you, Sam.

SAM: Bye, Jason.

SARAH: *(As she leaves, to Sam)* I can't believe you.

She erupts at him.

Never! Ever! Come near me ever again!

She begins to cry. Sarah and Jason exit, Sam is now alone in the street. He walks to centre-stage and sits down. He places his hands on his head and begins to cry.

SAM: Fuck.

Sam sits in the silence for a moment. Rain begins to trickle down on him. He looks up as the tears fall down his face. He looks at his bloody hand and cries. Lights from stage right indicate a car pulling up near Sam. A door opens and closes. Sam's sister, Violet enters.

VIOLET: Sam? Tony said you'd be here.

Sam looks up at his sister. He cries.

Sam, what's the matter?

Sam stands up. He walks towards his sister and hugs her. He cries on her shoulder as she comforts him.

SAM: I fucked up.

Violet consoles Sam.

VIOLET: It's okay. *(With concern)* What happened to your hand?

SAM: Punched the floor.

Violet laughs.

VIOLET: Idiot.

Sam now looks at his sister.

SAM: Everything is so fucked up. I don't know what I'm going to do.

Violet reassures Sam.

VIOLET: We're going to get you some help. Real help, and everything's going to be okay.

Sam starts to cry again. His sister hugs him tighter. She reassures him. She reassures her brother that he is okay. The lights fade. The rain stops. Scene ends.

Act Three

Scene one

Months later. Blackout, we hear a narration of Doctor Adams' voice.

DOCTOR ADAMS: What is it about being abandoned that scares you so much, Sam? Where do you think it comes from?

The lights brighten and we see Sam and Doctor Adams. Sitting opposite each other. In session. Sam is on stage left; he is sat on a chair slouched. Depressed. Doctor Adams is on stage right, she is upright with a pen and paper writing down, taking notes on what Sam is saying.

SAM: Um. Maybe from when I was a kid. I, uh. I was always left out. When I was younger. I guess. Maybe. The fear of a reoccurrence of that feeling of loneliness and abandonment. Maybe, that's what I'm scared of. All that. Repressed pain, coming back at me.

DOCTOR ADAMS: Okay. Good. It's good that you can recognise the pain. It's origin. What do you think triggers these memories? Brings them up for you.

SAM: I, um. I think maybe that for so long I've been scared of people leaving. And then it actually started to happen. You know? School ended. I lost touch with friends. My grandparents died. My mother died. My dad moved away.

He pauses, and sighs.

It just feels like. Everyone is leaving me.

Tears fill his eyes.

And I had no control. I couldn't handle it. It was all coming true. Everything I was scared of. Maybe – maybe the breakup I had. Triggered it all.

DOCTOR ADAMS: Well, there seems to be a pattern of reoccurring memories. Certain events of abandonment bring up past grief and maybe losses. It seems you suffered a lot of loss the past couple years.

SAM: *(Sniffles)* Yeah.

DOCTOR ADAMS: You haven't spoken much about your recent split with Sarah. Is that something that would frequently play on your mind?

SAM: Yeah. Yeah, it was. Very painful. It was a messy breakup, and we both said a lot of hurtful things to each other.

He pauses.

I guess there's a lot of guilt.

DOCTOR ADAMS: Okay. Guilt.

She pauses.

Okay. What is it exactly that you feel guilt over?

SAM: I wasn't the best boyfriend. Looking back, I can see my mistakes. I thought I was always doing the right thing but, what did I know? It was my first serious relationship and – I just felt so attached. So comforted by her. Maybe I relied on her too much.

DOCTOR ADAMS: Okay, interesting. Maybe your constant reliance on Sarah, put pressure on her because she didn't know how to deal with your problems, and that's where your guilt lies.

SAM: Exactly. But there's so much more guilt. I was so scared of her leaving. Of being abandoned or something happening to her, I would freak out every time she went to parties or out places. I was scared she'd cheat or find someone new. Someone better. Or what if she got hurt, I couldn't deal with losing her. I couldn't handle a loss like that.

DOCTOR ADAMS: When you say, 'A loss like that'. What do you mean?

He pauses and thinks.

SAM: If anything happened to her.

His voice begins to break.

I don't know if I would want to live anymore.

There is a silence in the room, Doctor Adams writes in her notebook.

DOCTOR ADAMS: Suicide. Is that something that you would think about?

SAM: Not so much anymore.

DOCTOR ADAMS: And, why's that the case?

SAM: I, uh. I-I tr-

He stops and collects himself.

I've attempted before.

Doctor Adams nods, in silence. She writes in her notebook.

DOCTOR ADAMS: Is that an experience you'd like to talk about?

Sam shakes his head. Tears trickle down his face. He looks to the ground in shame.

SAM: I think that, um. It's really hard, and I'm really ashamed. I'm so ashamed.

He stops and wipes his eyes.

I just got to a place, where I thought nobody cared. I was in a bad place with Sarah and my mum had just died.

A beat.

I just felt like nobody cared for me. I was so alone. I just can't really put into words the feeling and the state you're in when you just know that nobody in the world. Really, cares about you.

He sighs. He takes a moment.

When you don't add anything to any conversation, your life really means nothing. You make nobody happy, and don't impact anyone. You have absolutely no purpose. Alone. I couldn't handle it and I just.

A tear falls down Sam's face.

I wanted to end my life just so it would stop. I just wanted it all to stop. I just couldn't do it; it was too much. It was all just. Too. Much.

Sam hangs his head in shame.

I'm sorry.

Doctor Adams sighs. She writes in her notebook and looks at Sam with reassurance.

DOCTOR ADAMS: Suicide, and mental health. Struggles. Is nothing to be ashamed of Sam. Everybody feels it at some point in their life. An important factor you need to always remember is that there is so much love in this world. You are never, ever alone. You should be proud you are here. You beat it, you're here. Never be ashamed of that. It's okay to feel those feelings. It is normal.

SAM: *(Quietly)* I just feel like, I've let everyone down.

A beat.

When Sarah said I was selfish. She was right. It was selfish of me to try and end my life.

DOCTOR ADAMS: It's not selfish. Not at all. You were struggling. It's okay to struggle, Sam.

SAM: Yeah. Yeah I know. I guess I just never really saw it as struggling, and sort of-

He pauses to think.

I saw myself as a burden.

DOCTOR ADAMS: In what way?

SAM: You know, as in. Everything I did was burdening other people, I was ruining their days, their lives.

DOCTOR ADAMS: How were you ruining their lives?

Sam tries to hold back emotion.

SAM: I always hurt people. Hurt the people I love and want to protect. I end up being the person who hurts them.

DOCTOR ADAMS: Well, I'm sure that's not really the case. Your mind is telling you these things, Sam. Have you ever heard of core beliefs?

SAM: I haven't.

DOCTOR ADAMS: Well, when a thought in your head is so strong and so constant. It's ingrained in your mind. It's a constant belief, you constantly believe. It's your first response.

SAM: Well, how do I fix that? How do I make it not a core belief.

DOCTOR ADAMS: With a lot of talking. More of these sessions, Sam. We can do exercises to understand your thought pattern. Where these thoughts are originating in a stressful situation. We can analyse and understand situations where you feel this way. Once we understand them, we can start to change your thought pattern. Would that sound like something that would be helpful for you Sam?

SAM: Yeah, yes. Thank you, doctor.

DOCTOR ADAMS: So, we'll sign you up for more sessions?

Sam thinks. He eventually nods.

SAM: Yes.

Doctor Adams speaks but her voice is distorted, Sam is zoning out. He gets up slowly and walks to centre-stage. The lights dim down and there is a spotlight on Sam. He looks into the audience with a blank and depressed stare. There is nothing but tears in his eyes. There is nothing but blankness in his mind. The distorted sound of Doctor Adams' voice now turns into the sound of a busy street. The lights brighten and Sam is now on the busy street with people walking around. His phone rings. He reaches for his pocket and answers.

Hello?

There is a narration of Sarah's voice.

SARAH: *(Softly)* Hey. How was it? Are you alright?

SAM: Yeah, well I mean it was okay. It's tough, you know. It really makes you think, a lot to talk about it.

SARAH: I know, it's really hard but I'm so proud of you.

Sam. I love you.

SAM: Yeah, I love you too.

Sam moves towards stage right. Sarah enters from stage left.

SARAH: So, how have you been?

SAM: *(Jokingly)* Well, you know. Diagnosed with depression. Therapy once a week, rent went up. Cloud nine, Sarah.

Sarah laughs.

SARAH: Dick.

They both chuckle.

It's nice to hear you laugh. It's been a while.

SAM: Yeah, well. I'm sorry.

SARAH: No, Sam. No. Please don't apologise. You've nothing to be sorry for.

SAM: I can't help but feel guilty, you know? Doctor Adams said it's a core belief.

SARAH: Core belief?

SAM: A thought ingrained in your mind, that it's your automatic thought response.

SARAH: What's yours?

SAM: To always feel like it's my fault? I always hurt people. I feel a lot of guilt for just being here.

SARAH: I know, I know. I'm sorry this is all happening to you, Sam. I'm sorry about that night.

SAM: Yeah, well. Thank you for apologising. I don't want you to feel any guilt. It's not your fault I feel this way.

SARAH: I know.

She pauses.

Did you talk about your attempt? I think it's really important you mention it to her, Sam.

SAM: Yeah, we. We talked about it.

SARAH: *(Shocked)* Wow. I'm so proud of you. So incredibly proud. What did she say about it?

SAM: She just said I wasn't alone, and that it's okay and that it's normal.

Sarah sighs,

SARAH: It's okay, Sam. It's all going to be okay. Just remember okay. If you do anything stupid. You're just leaving us behind. Your family. Your friends. We all love you. We don't want to lose you, and you're not alone. Never.

Sam tears up.

SAM: Yeah, thank you. That means a lot, Sarah.

He pauses.

Do you think we could see each other this weekend? I'd like to talk. I'd like to see you.

SARAH: *(Surprised)* Oh. Well. I'm at a party this weekend. But. Maybe soon, yeah?

Sam absorbs the information. He is hurt. Almost like nothing has changed. He brushes off his feelings.

SAM: Ah. Well, that's okay, I think I'm working most of the weekend anyway.

There is a pause.

Have fun, though. I mean it.

SARAH: Alright. I have to go here; I need to cook dinner. Take care of yourself, okay? Are you heading home now?

SAM: No, I. I'm away to the pub here. To meet Tony and John.

A beat.

They were worried about me, so.

SARAH: That sounds lovely. Have a good time, okay.

SAM: Yeah, I will, thank you. I love you, Sarah.

SARAH: I love you, Sam.

They both hang up their phones, the lights fade, and the scene ends.

Scene two

In Sarah's house. She is preparing dinner for her family, Fiona enters.

FIONA: Hi, love. How are you feeling?

SARAH: All good. I'm just making chicken here is that okay?

FIONA: More than okay, sounds lovely.

There is a slight awkward silence, Fiona sits down at the dining table.

So, have you heard anything from Sam?

SARAH: Yeah. He had therapy today.

FIONA: How was it?

SARAH: He didn't really go much into it.

FIONA: Well, why not?

SARAH: I don't know. Can we leave it?

FIONA: Okay, okay. Sorry. I didn't mean to push it.

She pauses and thinks.

Have you packed for New York?

SARAH: Bits and pieces.

FIONA: Have you told Sam we're going?

SARAH: Why does everything have to be about Sam?

FIONA: Because we haven't talked about it, Sarah. What happened that night? What he did to himself. Is it over between you and Sam?

SARAH: I don't know.

FIONA: Why haven't you told him about New York?

SARAH: Did I say I didn't?

FIONA: *(Exploding)* Fuck, Sarah!

SARAH: *(Shocked)* Mummy!

FIONA: Why are you being so cryptic? This isn't you!

SARAH: I got drunk! Okay! He pushed me over and over again for years and then I finally snapped! Alright!

FIONA: *(Scoffs)* Jesus.

SARAH: What! What, mummy! What now!

Fiona sighs. Disappointed.

FIONA: Nothing. I have nothing to say.

SARAH: Good. I have guests coming over soon.

FIONA: Right.

Silence. There is clear tension in the room.

SARAH: You don't have to be short with me. It's a sensitive subject that's all. There's a lot of unaired feelings between the two of us. It's really hard.

FIONA: I know.

Sarah begs.

SARAH: Mummy, please.

FIONA: God, I don't know what you want from me Sarah. I'm trying.

She goes to leave, the doorbell rings.

Your guests are here.

SARAH: Yeah. Thanks.

FIONA: I'll let them in. We need to talk about this later.

Sarah sighs and she puts her hands on her head. Fiona exits to stage left; she opens the door and greets her friends. Annie, Laura, and Luke enter from stage left, Fiona leaves.

ANNIE: Hey, bitch!

LAURA: Hey!

Laura and Luke wave. Sarah greets them all. She picks up a remote and begins to play music.

LUKE: *(Approaching Sarah)* Hi. How are you?

SARAH: Hi, yeah. I'm doing okay.

LUKE: Let's catch up in a second here. I'm just going to go to the bathroom quickly.

SARAH: Yeah, no problem.

Luke sets down a bag containing gifts and exits to the bathroom. Laura approaches Sarah.

LAURA: Hey, how are you?

SARAH: Hi Laura, I'm okay. I'm doing alright, how've you been it's good to see you.

LAURA: I'm good, I'm good.

A beat.

I heard about you and Sam; I hope you're okay you two were with each other for ages.

SARAH: Yeah. Well, I'm trying to forget about him for now.

LAURA: Cheers to that. *(She chuckles)* Fuck him.

She grabs Annie, who is pouring cups of drinks.

Come on, fuck him!

ANNIE: *(Simultaneously)* Fuck Sam!

LAURA: *(Simultaneously)* Fuck Sam!

They all drink, Sarah laughs. Luke reappears and walks towards Sarah.

LUKE: Sounds like a cheers I can agree to.

SARAH: *(Laughing)* Luke!

LUKE: Who breaks up with *you* Sarah? No respectable man would.

Sarah laughs.

SARAH: No, I broke up with him.

LUKE: And you have never made a better decision.

Everyone laughs, Luke turns towards Annie and Laura.

Sorry, would you mind leaving us alone for a minute?

Annie and Laura both look at each other.

ANNIE: Oh, wow okay. Sorry for interrupting.

LAURA: We'll leave you two lovebirds alone.

They both laugh.

SARAH: Guys.

Annie and Laura exit, giggling with each other. There is a silent pause.

LUKE: Hm. Lovebirds.

SARAH: Yeah, I'm sorry about them two. They're just. Idiots.

LUKE: Yeah.

He pauses.

So, what are you drinking?

SARAH: *(Chuckling)* Fanta. And. Vodka. But, slightly more of the vodka than the Fanta.

Luke laughs.

LUKE: You must be joking, right? It's so light I thought you were drinking lemonade, or some fancy cocktail!

SARAH: *(Chuckling)* No. That's just how I like my drinks!

They both laugh. There is a pause for a moment. Luke's demeanour changes.

LUKE: Look, Sarah. I know we joke but I haven't seen you since the breakup. I just genuinely want to check up on how you are. I've been through it a lot myself and, it's tough. You definitely don't want to be on your own with this kind of stuff. I just want to check that you're okay.

SARAH: Yeah, sorry Luke. I don't really like talking about Sam. It's a sensitive subject, you know?

LUKE: Yeah, I understand that. I get it, I've had my fair share of rough breakups.

SARAH: Is that so, Luke?

LUKE: *(Chuckling)* Yeah, yeah. But you know what I mean. I just get how tough it can be. Maybe you should talk to me about how you're feeling. It's lonely sometimes.

Sarah sighs.

SARAH: Yeah. Really fucking lonely.

LUKE: Well, come on then. Talk to me.

SARAH: Fine! What kind of shit do you want to here?

LUKE: Oh. The whole lot.

They both laugh together. Sarah pauses and thinks for a minute.

SARAH: I guess. You know.

She laughs.

He was just fucking mean, and he was strict. He was always so uptight and. He was an asshole.

LUKE: *(Shocked)* Wow okay. I mean, get it out of your system.

She drinks her drink and slurs her words.

SARAH: He would just get drunk and swear at me and tell me how hard *his* boring life is! God forbid he ever did anything for me because holy fuck! You would never hear the end of it. Oh!

She mocks Sam.

'You know I'm the only reason you're in university! I bought this flat!' Like oh my god! Shut up!

LUKE: *(Chuckling)* He's a pure asshole, Sarah.

SARAH: He's such a hypocrite. He would tell me not to do one thing, oh don't get too drunk. Don't do these drugs, don't stay out too late. And he! He was loaded! Every! Fucking! Weekend!

LUKE: And he's a junkie too!

Sarah is obviously riled up. Luke sits closer to her and offers her comfort.

LUKE: Look, I know I joke around. But you've been through a lot with this guy. He's put you through hell.

SARAH: *(Regretfully)* Yeah.

Luke touches her cheek.

LUKE: I'm sorry you had to go through that.

They stare into each other's eyes for a moment. Sarah leans in and kisses Luke on the lips. She stops and looks at him in surprise.

SARAH: Fuck, I'm sorry.

LUKE: *(Startled)* N-No, please don't be sorry. It was nice.

Sarah backs away from Luke and begins to panic.

SARAH: Shit. *(Louder)* Shit!

Luke attempts to calm down Sarah.

LUKE: Hey, It's fine!

Laura and Annie enter again.

ANNIE: *(To Sarah)* What happened? Are you okay?

SARAH: Nothing. Guys, I'm sorry. I just. I need some space – I think it was all too soon.

LAURA: *(To Luke)* What happened?

LUKE: N-Nothing, nothing happened.

ANNIE: Okay, alright. Laura? Luke? Do you mind? I don't know. Going? It's just all very soon but thank you so much for coming it was nice to see you both.

Sarah places her hands on her head.

LAURA: Yeah, that's not a problem.

Laura grabs Luke's arm and pulls him out with her, gently.

LUKE: *(Leaving)* Shit, Sarah. I'm so sorry.

Laura and Luke exit. Annie walks over to the door and shuts it. They both stand in an awkward silence for a moment, looking at the ceiling and floor. Annie turns to Sarah.

ANNIE: Alright, what happened?

SARAH: *(Softly)* I kissed him.

ANNIE: *(Shocked)* Oh. Oh shit.

SARAH: Yeah! Oh Shit!

ANNIE: What are you going to do? You have to tell Sam.

SARAH: Fuck no!

ANNIE: Sarah! You have to. How would you feel if this was the other way round?

SARAH: We're not together anymore. I don't owe him shit.

ANNIE: Sarah, please. He's in the worst state of mind. He needs to find out from you. God knows what he might do.

Sarah sighs and looks at Annie. The look on her face changes.

SARAH: Right, fine. Jesus. Hand me the phone. Let's go meet him.

ANNIE: Okay. Good.

Annie lifts Sarah's phone from the table and passes it to her. She dials a number. The phone rings simultaneously with the lights dimming until they fade out. The scene ends.

Scene three

Annie and Sarah arrive to the smoking area of the local pub. Sarah checks her phone for any texts or calls from Sam. Suddenly Sam appears from stage right. He stumbles in and slurs his words. He is visibly drunk. He locks eye contact with Sarah.

SAM: Hi. What are you doing here?

She pauses. She looks at him.

SARAH: Sam. I need to tell you something.

SAM: Well. Can it wait? I'm drinking. With Tony, and John. *(To Annie)* You remember Tony?

ANNIE: Yeah. Sam, this is serious.

SAM: *(Chuckling to himself)* Fuck. Who died?

   Sarah looks at Sam with concern. Tears begin to fill Sarah's eyes. Suddenly, Sam's demeanour changes.

SARAH: *(Softly)* Sam.

SAM: Yeah.

   He pauses, trying to collect himself.

I know what you're going to say.

ANNIE: What?

SARAH: *(Confused)* What are you saying, Sam? What do you mean you know?

   Sam sits on a stool next to him. He pauses and lights a cigarette. He takes a draw.

SAM: I bumped into Luke, earlier.

   Sarah's face drops.

ANNIE: Shit.

SARAH: *(Trying to reach out to him)* Sam.

   Sam refuses to take Sarah's hand. He continues to speak.

SAM: He said some very interesting things. He was coming over to your house. For a party. That you practically begged him to come.

SARAH: No. No, it wasn't like that at all Sam. I promise. Luke's my friend I haven't seen him in ages.

SAM: He made it very clear to me that you and him were going to get. *(He turns to Annie)* And I quote, 'Intimate.' Apparently.

Annie and Sarah are both equally shocked as each other.

SARAH: What! No!

ANNIE: Jesus.

Sam laughs to himself.

SAM: *(Laughing)* He bought fucking condoms.

SARAH: Oh my god!

ANNIE: What the actual fuck.

They all pause, thinking to themselves.

SARAH: Sam. I- don't know what to say.

Sam looks blankly at Sarah. He takes a draw from his cigarette.

SAM: You fuck him?

SARAH: *(Frustrated)* No, Sam! I did not have sex with Luke!

SAM: What did you do then? It doesn't take a fucking scientist to analyse that guilty look on your face.

ANNIE: Sam, lay off her. You're drunk.

SAM: *(With aggression)* Who put some balls on you. This is nothing to do with you!

Sarah fights back at Sam.

SARAH: Sam! Oh my god!

SAM: *(Still, shouting at Annie)* This is nothing to do with you! You fucking bitch!

Annie laughs. Sarah pushes Sam.

SARAH: Sam!

ANNIE: *(To Sam)* Fuck you!

Sam screams in Sarah's face. Towering over her. She backs away. Afraid of him

SAM: *(Screaming)* What did you do then!

He is seething with anger.

Tell me!

There is a pause. Sarah stares at Sam in fear. Annie stands to the side in shock. Sam backs away. He realises what he has done. His face drops. The colour runs from his face.

SAM: *(Softly)* I'm sorry.

There is silence for a moment. They all catch their breath. Sarah snaps at Sam.

SARAH: *(Sharply)* Don't. You ever! Get fucking violent with me ever again, Sam. Don't you dare talk to Annie like that ever again!

She pauses. She wants to hurt him.

I kissed him. I kissed him, and I don't regret it Sam!

He laughs and stares at Sarah. He looks at Annie for a split second then back at Sarah. Tears fill his eyes. He takes a draw from his cigarette and turns his back from the girls. He hides his real feelings. He laughs.

SAM: Pathetic. Just a kiss? I did more with a girl in the bar about twenty minutes ago. If you're going to get with someone else, especially Luke. You could at least have fucked him. He's been gagging for it for at least a year.

Annie and Sarah burst out laughing in shock.

SARAH: *(Screaming)* Oh my god! What the actual fuck!

Sam snaps back.

SAM: How was I supposed to react, did you not hear what Luke said to me?

ANNIE: *(Shouting, to Sam)* It was all lies Sam!

SAM: *(Shouting back)* You think I'm fucking psychic?

Sarah laughs at Sam. There are tears in her eyes. She is hurt.

SARAH: So, you went and immediately fucked some girl? You're even more of a piece of shit than I thought you were.

SAM: Alright, Sarah. Just fuck off.

Annie's anger with Sam now boils. She approaches him.

ANNIE: You are unbelievable Sam. You know, I see the real you now. All this nice guy act has been dropped. I see who you really are.

She laughs. Sam gives her a cold stare.

You're a nasty, violent man. We're only here because *I* wanted to spare your feelings. This is the thanks I get?

Sam scoffs.

SAM: Do you want me to say it again? Go fuck yourself.

SARAH: *(To Sam)* Oh my god, I actually hate you.

SAM: Go fuck yourself too, Sarah. I'm leaving.

He tries to walk away; Sarah grabs his arm.

SARAH: No! You just don't get to walk away from me Sam!

He pulls his arm away.

SAM: Watch me, Sarah.

She tries to hurt him.

SARAH: I never want to see your face again Sam!

A beat.

I'm moving to New York next week.

There is a pause. Sam is shocked.

SAM: Since when?

SARAH: Like that fucking matters to you.

Sam laughs. He is done with the situation.

SAM: Alright, Sarah. Whatever. Good for you. Go to fucking New York. Hope you choke on the fumes.

Sam tries to walk away again, Sarah shouts after him.

SARAH: *(Shouting)* You know what Sam. I hope you die! I hope you slit your wrists and fucking die!

Silence. Sarah breathes heavy. Annie is silent. Shocked. Sam stops, he faces away from Sarah. He hangs is head down. He can't believe she has said what she did. He is hurt. The most he has ever been.

SAM: *(Softly)* Wow.

A beat.

Wow, Sarah. Well, you've completely outdone yourself this time.

He turns to face her.

Out of everything you could've said to me. You said the most hurtful thing you could possibly imagine.

Sarah begins to cry. The atmosphere is awkward. Tense.

ANNIE: *(Softly, to Sarah)* Sarah.

Sarah stands still, breathing heavily.

SAM: You know what Sarah. You know that's a painful memory for me. Ever since then, you've been acting like you care. That you're here for me.

A beat.

For a split second I thought you changed. But you're still just the cold-hearted bitch you always were.

Sarah cries.

I'm glad you're going to New York. I don't want any contact from you. I don't ever want to see your face again.

Sam reaches in his pocket. He pulls out a key and tosses it to Sarah.

Move your shit out of the apartment. Soon as you can. Preferably when I'm not there. Then go to New York, and never fucking speak to me again.

Sam walks away, he sobs to himself.

SARAH: *(Crying, shouting to Sam)* We're done Sam. We're done forever. You fucking hear me?!

SAM: *(Walking away, back inside to the bar at stage right)* Goodbye, Sarah.

Sam slams the bar door shut. He exits. Sarah breaks down crying.

ANNIE: Come on. Let's go.

SARAH: *(Crying)* I'm sorry. I'm sorry.

ANNIE: Let's just get you home.

Annie grabs Sarah and they both exit. The lights fade on a grim and bleak atmosphere of the intense argument. Scene ends.

Scene four

In Sam's apartment, the following week. The apartment is now messier than it was before. Sam lies on the sofa holding his head. John enters the apartment with cups of coffee and startles him, waking him up.

SAM: *(Startled)* Jesus! Do you just not knock anymore?

JOHN: Never know with you these days. Got to be careful. Might've done something stupid.

John sets a cup of coffee down on a table.

Here, drink this. It'll help your head.

SAM: *(Drinking the coffee)* Thanks.

John sits beside Sam on the sofa. He switches on the TV.

JOHN: Is Sarah coming over to grab a few more things for New York?

SAM: I don't know. We talked briefly.

JOHN: *(Chuckling)* I'm not surprised. How did you manage to de-rail the situation to a state like that?

SAM: I was hammered.

Sam holds his head and groans. John sighs.

JOHN: Look. You shouldn't end things like that. I know she said some pretty messed up things, but. You owe it to each other to talk it out before she moves.

Sam thinks.

SAM: Yeah, I know. I should. It was just really bad the last time we talked.

A beat.

I really hurt her. I don't want to do that again.

JOHN: You won't. You need closure.

SAM: *(Sighing)* Part of me just feels that it's best if I just disappear. Leave her alone forever. Where she can't be hurt by me ever again. You know, I was a *terrible* fucking partner. She deserves to get away as far as possible from me.

JOHN: That's not true. That's not true, you're being hard on yourself.

SAM: No, you don't know that.

JOHN: You're human, Sam. No one is perfect. Everyone is a dick at times. You owe it to yourself to tell her how you really feel. You don't want your last memory of you together to be a drunken mess of an interaction.

Sam pauses.

SAM: Jesus, I really was. I mean, I apologised but. I can tell she's still really hurt. I just can't handle myself. I can't deal with my emotions.

JOHN: Don't be hard on yourself.

John stops. He sighs.

You still haven't really said much about what happened. I don't want to find you like that again.

Sam hangs his head.

SAM: I'm sorry for putting you through that.

JOHN: I'm just glad you're alive. But please talk to me. Try to make me understand how you got to that place. Maybe I can prevent it from happening again. Spot the signs and shit.

SAM: Wow, well I mean. It's long. Like, I wasn't always feeling low. It just kind of crept up on me.

A beat.

Me and Sarah. We were so attached. Genuinely, I think anyone who knew us could tell that. I based, every feeling of mine off of hers'. I was happy when she was happy with me. If she was mad at me, I'd feel awful about myself. I don't even know. I think when it got to summer, and her image of me really changed. She no longer was besotted by me or saw me as this wonderful man.

He tries to collect himself.

She could see I was *deeply* flawed. That's when it all took a nosedive, I think. Starting my job that was so new. I couldn't adapt like school or university, I just. I felt so isolated.

Silence. John listens.

Eventually everything just got bleaker. Grey. I couldn't sleep. I couldn't eat. I went days without sleep. I lost so much weight. The colour of everything was drained out. The more distant she grew from me the worse it got. I cried every day. Every night. I couldn't focus on work. I didn't enjoy anything. I distanced myself from friends. Acquaintances. Eventually I just. Only saw one way out.

The silence in the room is deafening. John has tears in his eyes. He hugs Sam and reassures him.

JOHN: Everything is going to be okay.

The two hug for longer. Two best friends. Connected.

(Softly) It's not your fault.

There is a long silence in the room.

SAM: Sometimes I think that it is.

John looks at Sam. He nods. He sighs.

JOHN: We need out of the flat. Fancy some golf?

SAM: *(Laughing, as the tears trickle down his face)* Golf?

JOHN: Well, Tony arranged it, don't look at me.

SAM: I don't think I'm a big golf fan.

JOHN: No. No excuses. Get up. Get a coat on and let's go. Don't be so down in the dumps.

SAM: *(Getting up)* You're a dick, you know that. But I love you.

JOHN: That I have never denied. And I love you too mate.

John stands up.

SAM: But thank you. You're surprisingly good with your words.

JOHN: *(Walking out)* Don't I fucking know it.

The two men laugh with each other as they leave the apartment. Time passes throughout the day; the sun sets out the window. It is now evening. Sarah and Fiona arrive at the door. They enter the apartment to collect some of Sarah's items before leaving. They walk around the apartment.

FIONA: Bit of a dump.

SARAH: Yeah. It wasn't like this when I was living here. He's a bit out of control on his own.

FIONA: Yeah, well I can see.

SARAH: *(Laughing)* The TV's still on!

FIONA: *(Laughing, as well)* My god! Right, what are we getting darling.

SARAH: Just. A few coats and shoes. They're in our room can you grab them for me? I'm just going to look around here and see if there's anything stupid I've left behind.

FIONA: Alright. *(Laughing)* Good luck with that! *(Walking away)* State of the place, honestly.

Fiona exits to Sam and Sarah's old bedroom. Sarah walks around the apartment, looking at pictures on the wall. Holding picture frames, she smiles as she reminisces on her relationship with Sam. She picks up a t-shirt of Sam's and smells it. She smiles. She looks around the room as if she misses it. As if she misses Sam. A tear falls from Sarah's face. She wipes it away as Fiona re-enters, holding two coats over her arm and a pair of shoes.

FIONA: That's all I could find. Do you think that'll do?

SARAH: Yeah, no I think it'll be fine. That's all I need really, to be honest with you.

Fiona notices that Sarah is upset.

FIONA: What's wrong?

SARAH: *(Quickly)* No. No. I'm fine.

FIONA: *(With concern)* It's okay. It's normal.

Fiona walks towards Sarah and gives her a hug.

It's normal to be back here and be flooded with emotions. You lived here for years.

SARAH: It's just overwhelming. I feel like I'm making a mistake.

FIONA: I know, I know. But our new life in New York is such a fantastic opportunity. Really. I promise you you're not making a mistake walking away from this life. It's what you need. I promise you.

SARAH: Are you sure?

FIONA: I promise you, darling. Now, come on. Let's get you out of here. Our flight's later on today anyway.

SARAH: *(Sniffling)* Yeah, yeah. You go on ahead. I just want five more minutes.

Fiona pauses, then smiles.

FIONA: Alright, darling. I'll see you soon.

She turns around and exits the apartment. The lights on stage right dim. Sarah sits down on the sofa. She looks at the table and sees an envelope. She picks it up and realises her name is written on it. She opens it up to find there is a letter inside written by Sam. The lights on stage right brighten. Sam is leaning on a table, smoking a cigarette. He is not there, but in Sarah's mind. He begins to narrate the letter as Sarah reads.

SAM: *(Narrating, he speaks with sincerity)* Sarah. I hope you're doing okay. I wish we had more time to talk about all of our problems, but. I realise that, maybe that isn't the best approach. I know that I need closure, but seeing you will only hurt you, if not make you want to stay. So, I wrote a letter. I know we don't speak anymore. I don't know if we'll ever speak again. If that's the case. I just want you to know how I feel. What I want to say to you. For the final time. I've really missed talking to you. I'm genuinely so sorry about how I spoke to you last week and throughout our entire relationship. I was immature, stupid, and an angry person. I was wrong. And I'm so sorry. I can't fix my mental health. Not right now. It's going to take time for me to fully heal. Now, I realise I wasn't fixed the whole time we were together. I was always broken. I couldn't take care of myself, and I couldn't take care of you. I hurt you. I'm so sorry. I want you to be happier. I want you to live your life and find a husband who will give you beautiful kids and will allow you to raise them the way you dream. I want you to go to New York, go as far away from here as possible. Sarah. I love you. I loved you since you made me feel safe, and comforted, and warm. You are the complete definition of love to me, Sarah. I ruined us. I poisoned us, I hurt you and your family. The best thing I can do is to be as far away as possible from you so that's why you need to let me go. You need to let me, let you go. And if I don't write this letter and I talk to you face to face, I'll never be able to walk away. You are funny, you are caring, you are loving. You care for people, and you are there for people – whether they deserve it or not. You're always there. No matter what. Ready to help. You cared for me.

You accepted me, you protected me. You *loved* me. Part of me will never know why you said that to me last week. Heat of the moment. Pent up rage. I don't know. I know you didn't mean it though. You could have. You were there when I went through those dark periods of my life, you *felt* them with me. You experienced that pain. I forgive you Sarah, okay. I forgive you for all of it. I don't hate you; I don't dislike you. I know we give each other glares and looks when we bump into each other. But I'll never forget the looks we used to share. I could never hate you. I don't hold any wrong doings against you. I don't hold anything you've said against you. I don't hold it against you in any way. I *love* you.

Sam walks to the door, he opens it, he has one foot out the door, Sarah looks at him. She cries.

I love you, Sarah. No matter what. No matter how far away you are. I love you. Always.

Sam flicks the light switch on the wall, and gently closes the door. The set is in darkness. Sam is comforted in his friends. Sarah lives her new life in New York. They are separate, but they are always connected, scene ends. Blackout.

"Connections" is based on real life events.

Please take care of yourself. If you're struggling in a relationship, or with your mental health. Please seek the help you need and talk to the people you trust the most. Take note and seek help from these helplines if needed. Please remember. You are never alone. You are always loved. -T

Samaritans, 116 123.

National Suicide Prevention Helpline UK, 0800 689 5652.

Shout. If you would prefer not to talk, text SHOUT to 85258.

National Domestic Abuse Helpline, 0808 2000 247.

Women's Aid Online Chat, www.chat.womensaid.org,uk.

The Men's Advice Line, 0808 801 0327.

Victim Support, 0808 168 9111.

Connections supports Women's Aid ABCLN.

Women's Aid ABCLN, 028 256 32136

24hr Domestic and Sexual Abuse Helpline, 0808 802 1414

In an emergency, always call 999.

© TM Publishings, 2025

ISBN 978-1-0682436-0-8